Published By Nicholas Thompson

@ Lewis Eaton

Pegan Diet for Busy Professionals: Time-

saving Tips

ISBN 978-87-94477-47-5

TABLE OF CONTENTS

Cashew Yogurt

Ingredients:

- 1 tbsp of coconut oil

- 1 tsp of vanilla extract

- 2 tbsp of lemon juice

- ½ cup filtered water

- 2 cups of cashews, soaked for 3 hours minimum

- 1 ripe banana, cut into discs

- 1 tsp of psyllium husks in ½ cup of filtered water

- Pinch of sea salt

Directions:

1. Mix the psyllium husks with the water and set them aside to allow them to thicken.
2. Drain the water from the cashews before placing them in the blender. Add the vanilla, lemon juice, coconut oil, salt, and banana before blending slowly as you add ½ a cup of water.
3. If the mixture isn't completely smooth yet, start to add water a tablespoon at a time until it becomes creamy and thick.
4. Pour this mixture into a bowl then stir in the thickened psyllium husks.
5. Set aside in the fridge for 30 minutes before using.
6. This yogurt can be used to make parfaits or simply enjoyed with a side of fresh fruit.

Oven-Roasted Eggs With Tomatoes And Asparagus

Ingredients:

- 2 tbsp olive oil

- 2 lbs asparagus

- Salt to taste

- 4 eggs

- 2 tsp fresh thyme, chopped

- 1 lb cherry tomatoes

- Pepper to taste

Directions:

1. Preheat the oven to 400 °F and grease a baking sheet.

2. Lie the asparagus side by side in an even layer and scatter the cherry tomatoes across them.

Drizzle the vegetables with salt, pepper, thyme, and olive oil.

3. Roast the vegetables for about 10–12 minutes until the asparagus is becoming tender and the tomatoes are wrinkling.

4. Remove the vegetables from the oven and add the eggs on top before seasoning with salt and pepper.

5. Return the baking sheet to the oven and bake for about 7–8 minutes until the white of the eggs are set yet the yolks are not.

6. Divide the contents of the baking sheet by four then serve.

Mock Overnight Oats

Ingredients:

- 1 tbsp almond butter

- 1 cup raspberries

- ⅓ cup chia seeds

- 1 tsp vanilla extract

- 1 cup coconut milk

- 3 tbsp maple syrup

- 1 cup cashew milk or almond milk

- ½ cup coconut flakes, unsweetened

Directions:

1. In a large bowl add the cashew milk, chia seeds, coconut milk, coconut flakes, vanilla extract, and maple syrup then mix thoroughly.

2. Let the mixture sit resting for a few minutes.

3. In the jars, create a layer of the mixture followed by raspberries then almond butter, and continue until all the Ingredients: have been used.

4. Refrigerate overnight and enjoy this meal for breakfast the following day.

Cherry-Hemp Smoothie

Ingredients:

- 75 g frozen pitted sweet cherries

- 2 tablespoons hemp seeds

- 1 tablespoon hemp oil

- 375 ml unsweetened Almond Milk

- ½ teaspoon ground ginger

Directions:

1. Combine all the Ingredients: in a blender and blend on high speed until smooth and creamy, about 45 seconds. Drink immediately.

Peachy Green Smoothie

Ingredients:

- 150 g frozen or canned sliced peaches

- 2 tablespoons almond butter

- 1 tablespoon chia seeds

- 500 ml unsweetened Almond Milk, chilled

- 2 teaspoons spirulina

Directions:

1. Combine all the Ingredients: in a blender and blend on high speed until smooth and creamy, about 45 seconds. Drink immediately.

Banana-Raspberry-Coconut Smoothie

Ingredients:

- 120 g frozen raspberries

- 2 tablespoons coconut butter 1 tablespoon coconut oil

- 250 ml coconut water (or filtered water), chilled 1 banana, peeled and frozen

- 60 g baby spinach

Directions:

1. Combine all the Ingredients: in a blender and blend on high speed until smooth and creamy, about 45 seconds. Drink immediately.

Flank Steak With Salad And A Homemade Vinaigrette

Ingredients:

- ¼ cup chopped herbs

- 1 clove garlic, minced

- 3 cups chopped lettuce

- 2 chopped plum tomatoes

- 2 3 oz. Flank steak

- 2/3 cup extra-virgin olive oil

- ¼ teaspoon red wine vinegar

- 1 teaspoon steak seasoning

Directions:

1. Mix together olive oil, red wine vinegar, chopped herbs, minced garlic; cover and sit in refrigerator.
2. Combine lettuce and tomatoes; chill.
3. Bring steaks to room temp, season and grill steaks 4-5 minutes per side.

Chicken Fajita Salad

Ingredients:

- ½ tablespoon lime juice

- 1 tablespoons chili powder

- 1 teaspoon ground cumin

- 1 teaspoon ground coriander

- 1 teaspoon brown sugar

- ¼ teaspoon cayenne pepper

- ½ pound stir fry chicken strips

- 1 bell pepper, julienned

- 4 cups shredded lettuce

- 2-3 diced tomatoes

- 1 can organic black beans, washed

- 4-5 gluten free pita chips

Directions:

1. In a plastic bag combine chicken strips, lime juice, chili powder, ground cumin, coriander, brown sugar, cayenne pepper.

2. Combine lettuce, tomatoes, and black beans then let chill in refrigerator.

3. Sauté chicken and peppers in skillet over olive oil 1-2 minutes; add to lettuce, tomatoes, and black beans and toss. mount per serving

Spinach & H2y Turkey Pita

Ingredients:

- ½ cup baby spinach leaves

- 1/3 cup bell pepper, diced

- 2 teaspoons organic h2y

- 2 4-inch whole wheat pitas

- 2 cups leftover shredded turkey

- 1 teaspoon walnuts

Directions:

1. In a small bowl mix together shredded turkey, diced bell peppers, h2y, and walnuts.
2. Fill each pita shell with half of baby spinach leaves then fill with half of turkey mixture.

Cinnamon And Coconut Porridge

Ingredients:

- 2 tablespoons flaxseed meal

- 1 tablespoon butter

- 1 and ½ teaspoon stevia

- 1 teaspoon cinnamon

- 2 cups of water

- 1 cup 36% heavy cream

- ½ cup unsweetened dried coconut, shredded

- Salt to taste

- Toppings as blueberries

Directions:

1. Add the listed Ingredients: to a small pot, mix well

2. Transfer pot to stove and place it over medium-low heat

3. Bring to mix to a slow boil

4. Stir well and remove the heat

5. Divide the mix into equal servings and let them sit for 10 minutes

6. Top with your desired toppings, and enjoy!

2-Skillet Kale And Avocado

Ingredients:

- 5 ounces fresh kale, stemmed and sliced into ribbons

- 1 avocado, sliced

- 4 large whole eggs

- 2 tablespoons olive oil, divided

- 2 cups mushrooms, sliced

- Salt and pepper as needed

Directions:

1. Take a large skillet and place it over medium heat

2. Add a tablespoon of olive oil

3. Add mushrooms to the pan and Saute for 3 minutes

4. Take a medium bowl and massage kale with the remaining 1 tablespoon olive oil (for about 1-2 minutes)

5. Add kale to skillet and place them on top of mushrooms

6. Place slices of avocado on top of the kale

7. Create 4 wells for eggs and crack each egg onto each hold

8. Season eggs with salt and pepper

9. Cover skillet and cook for 5 minutes

10. Serve hot!

Cool Tomato And Cucumber Gazpacho

Ingredients:

- 1 medium cucumber, coarsely chopped

- ½ cup extra virgin olive oil

- 1 tablespoon balsamic/red wine vinegar

- Salt and pepper as needed

- 8 ripe plum/heirloom tomatoes

- 1 medium red bell pepper, seeded and coarsely chopped

- Sunflower seeds for garnish

Directions:

1. Take your food processor and add tomatoes, pepper, cucumber, and pulse until everything breaks down

2. While the motor is still running, add oil, the
    process for about 2 minutes until the mix is
    smooth and velvety

3. Add vinegar and process for a few seconds
    more

4. Refrigerate the soup for about 2 hours, serve
    cold with a bit of salt and pepper

5. Garnish with some seeds if desired

6. **Enjoy!**

Warm Maple And Cinnamon Quinoa

Ingredients:

- 1 cup quinoa, rinsed

- 1 teaspoon cinnamon

- 1/4 cup chopped pecans

- 1 cup unsweetened nondairy milk

- 1 cup water

- 2 tablespoons pure maple syrup or agave

Directions:

1. Bring the almond milk, water, and quinoa to a boil. Lower the heat to medium-low and cover. Cook gently until the quinoa softens, about 15 minutes.

2. Turn off the heat and allow sitting, covered, for 5 minutes. Stir in the cinnamon, pecans, and syrup. Serve hot.

Spiced Orange Breakfast Couscous

Ingredients:

- 1 teaspoon ground cinnamon

- 1/4 teaspoon ground cloves

- 1/2 cup dried fruit

- 3 cups orange juice

- 1.1/2 cups couscous

- 1/2 cup chopped almonds

Directions:

1. Take the orange juice to a boil. Add the couscous, cinnamon, and cloves and remove from heat. Shield the pan and allow sitting until the -couscous softens.

2. Fluff the couscous and stir in the dried fruit and nuts. Serve -immediately. Pecans and syrup. Serve hot.

Breakfast Parfaits

Ingredients:

- 1 cup granola

- 1/2 cup walnuts

- 2 14-ounce cans of coconut milk, refrigerated overnight

- 1 cup sliced strawberries or other seasonal berries

Directions:

1. Pour off the canned coconut milk liquid and retain the solids.

2. In 3 parfait glasses, layer the coconut milk solids, granola, walnuts, and -strawberries. Serve immediately.

Instant Pot Vegan Pho

INGREDIENTS::

- 1/2 teaspoon ground clove

- 1 tablespoon garlic

- 1 teaspoon ground ginger

- 1 cinnamon stick

- 1 white onion, quartered

- 2 (28-ounce) cans vegetable broth

- 1 1/2 cups shiitake mushrooms

- Fine mesh sieve

- Pho bowls

- Reusable chopsticks

- Vietnamese Instant Pot cookbook

- Vegan pho broth recipe

- 1 tablespoon olive oil

- 10 whole black peppercorns

- 3 whole star anise

- 1 baby bok choy

- 6 spring onions

- 1 teaspoon salt

- 8.8 ounce package thin rice noodles

- Pho soup Toppings

- Lime

- Jalapeno

- Spring onions/Chives

DIRECTIONS:

1. Place instant pot on sauté mode. Add in olive oil, black peppercorns, star anise, clove, garlic, ginger, and the cinnamon stick. Sauté about 3 minutes.

2. Add in quartered onion and sauté another two minutes. Turn off sauté mode.

3. Pour in vegetable broth. Add in mushrooms. Add in spring onion bottoms reserving the chives for topping later. Pull the baby bok choy apart and wash. Add to pot. Add in salt and stir well.

4. Place lid onto the instant pot. Set valve to seal position. Press high pressure/pressure cook/manual button and set time to 1 minute. The broth will heat up as it comes to pressure.

5. Meanwhile, cook the rice noodles as direct on the stove. These have special instructions and shouldn't be made in the pot.

6. Once complete add the noodles to the pho. Serve with limes, jalapeno, cilantro, and any other toppings.

Paleo Vegan Pancakes

INGREDIENTS:

- 1/4 tsp. sea salt

- 2/3 cup unsweetened almond milk

- 2 tsp. apple cider vinegar

- 1 Tbsp. maple syrup

- 1 Tbsp. coconut oil, melted

- 1 cup almond flour

- 3/4 cup tapioca flour

- 1 Tbsp. baking powder

- 1 tsp. pure vanilla extract

DIRECTIONS:

1. Combine all of the Ingredients: in a blender. Blend for a few seconds then stop blender

and scrape sides and blend for a few seconds longer. You may also make the batter in a bowl however, blending does help to make these egg-free pancakes fluffier as stated above.

2. If needed, add additional liquid or flour in small increments (1/2 Tbsp. at a time) to achieve pancake batter consistency.

3. On medium/medium high heat pour batter on a greased skillet, about a scant 1/4 cup of batter per pancake.

4. Flip when pancakes begin to bubble or spatula easily slips under pancake. Continue to cook until golden brown on both sides.

5. Allow pancakes to cool slightly before enjoying.

6. Top the desired toppings such as Roasted Strawberry Vanilla Bean Sauce and nut butter.

Lemon Garlic Shrimp With Broccoli And Zucchini Noodles

INGREDIENTS:

- ⅛ teaspoon crushed red pepper flakes, or to taste

- Freshly ground black pepper

- 6–8 ounces wild large or extra-large shrimp, peeled and deveined with tails on (fresh or frozen and thawed), I used 9 shrimp.

- 2 cups broccoli florets (size the broccoli so it will cook in the same amount of time as shrimp)*

- 4 cups spiralized zucchini noodles (optional "sweat" with 1/2 teaspoon Celtic sea salt)*

- 2 tablespoons lemon juice

- 1/4 cup chopped parsley

- 1 tablespoon ghee or grass fed unsalted butter

- 1 tablespoon extra-virgin olive oil

- 4 garlic cloves, minced

- ½ cup chicken or vegetable broth or white wine

- 1/2 teaspoon Celtic sea salt, or to taste

- Vegan parmesan or parmesan cheese (optional)

DIRECTIONS:

1. In a large skillet, melt ghee or butter with olive oil. Add garlic and sauté on medium low until fragrant, about 1 minute.

2. Add broth, salt, red pepper flakes and a large pinch of black pepper and bring to a simmer.

3. Simmer the stock for about 2 minute to develop flavors.

4. Add shrimp and broccoli. Sauté on medium turning the shrimp once, until they just turn pink and the broccoli is bright green, 2 to 4 minutes depending upon their size.

5. Add the zucchini noodles, parsley and lemon.

6. Toss the noodles with the shrimp so they are coated with the garlic-lemon sauce. Heat just until warmed through, 1 minute. (Do not overcook or the zucchini noodles will become mushy.)

7. Sprinkle with parsley and vegan or regular parmesan.

Zucchini Fritters

Ingredients:

- 1 garlic clove, minced

- 1 tablespoon nutritional yeast

- 1 tablespoon fresh parsley, chopped

- 1 teaspoon lemon zest

- Salt and pepper to taste

- 2 cups grated zucchini

- ¼ cup almond flour

- 2 green onions, chopped

- Olive oil for frying

Directions:

1. Place grated zucchini in a clean kitchen towel and squeeze out excess moisture.

2. In a mixing bowl, combine zucchini, almond flour, green onions, garlic, nutritional yeast, parsley, lemon zest, salt, and pepper. Mix well.

3. In a skillet over medium heat, heat the olive oil.

4. Scoop tablespoon-sized portions of the mixture and flatten into fritters. Flatten tablespoon-sized amounts of the mixture into fritters. Fry until golden brown on both sides in a skillet.

5. Remove from heat and pat dry with a paper towel with any excess oil.

6. Serve warm.

Roasted Chickpeas

Ingredients:

- 1 teaspoon ground cumin

- ½ teaspoon paprika

- ½ teaspoon garlic powder

- 1 can chickpeas, drained and rinsed

- 1 tablespoon olive oil

- Salt and pepper to taste

Directions:

1. Preheat the oven to 400°F (200°C).
2. Using a paper towel, pat the chickpeas dry.
3. In a bowl, toss the chickpeas with olive oil, cumin, paprika, garlic powder, salt, and pepper until well coated.

4. Place the chickpeas on a baking sheet in a single layer.

5. Roast in the oven for 25-30 minutes, shaking the pan occasionally for even cooking.

6. Remove from the oven and let them cool slightly before enjoying the crispy roasted chickpeas.

Chocolate Avocado Mousse

Ingredients:

- ¼ cup maple syrup

- 2 tbsp almond milk (or other plant-based milk)

- 1 teaspoon vanilla extract

- Pinch of salt

- 2 ripe avocados

- ¼ cup unsweetened cocoa powder

- Fresh berries for garnish

Directions:

1. Scoop out the flesh of the avocados and place it in a blender or food processor.

2. Add cocoa powder, maple syrup, almond milk, vanilla extract, and a pinch of salt.

3. Blend on high until smooth and creamy, scraping down the sides as needed.

4. Place the mousse in individual serving glasses or bowls.

5. Refrigerate the mousse for at least 1 hour to allow it to set.

6. Before serving, garnish with fresh berries. Enjoy the rich and indulgent chocolate avocado mousse.

<h1 style="text-align:center">Vegan Black Bean Chili</h1>

Ingredients:

- 2 green bell pepper, diced

- 3 medium carrots, diced

- 2 jalapeño pepper, seeded and minced (optional, for heat)

- 3 tablespoons chilli powder

- 2 tablespoon of ground cumin

- 2 teaspoon of smoked paprika

- 2 teaspoon of dried oregano

- 2 can (15 ounces) of diced tomatoes

- 3 cans (15 ounces each) of black beans, rinsed and drained

- 2 can (15 ounces) of corn kernels, drained

- 2 cups vegetable broth

- 3 tablespoons of olive oil

- 2 large onion, chopped

- 4 cloves garlic, minced

- 2 red bell pepper, diced

- Salt and pepper to taste

- Fresh cilantro, chopped (for garnish)

- Lime wedges (for serving)

Directions:

1. Heat the olive oil in a large pot or Dutch oven over medium heat. Add the onion, garlic, bell peppers, carrots, and jalapeño (if using). Sauté for about 5 minutes until the vegetables start to soften.

2. Stir in the chilli powder, cumin, smoked paprika, and oregano.

3. Add the diced tomatoes, black beans, corn, and vegetable broth to the pot. Stir well to combine all the Ingredients:.

4. Bring the mixture to a boil, then reduce the heat to low and cover the pot.

5. Simmer the chilli for about 30 minutes, stirring occasionally. If the chilli becomes too thick, add more vegetable broth or water to reach your desired consistency.

6. Season with salt and pepper to taste. Adjust the spices if needed.

7. Remove the pot from the heat. Serve the vegan black bean chilli hot, garnished with fresh cilantro. Provide lime wedges on the side for squeezing over the chilli, if desired.

Butternut Squash And Kale Salad With Maple-Balsamic Dressing

Ingredients:

- 4 cups kale, stems removed and leaves thinly sliced

- 1/2 cup dried cranberries

- 1/4 cup toasted pumpkin seeds

- 1/4 cup crumbled feta cheese

- 2 small butternut squash, peeled, seeded, and cut into 1-inch cubes

- 2 tablespoon of olive oil

- Salt and pepper to taste

For the Maple-Balsamic Dressing:

- 2 clove of garlic, minced

- 1/4 cup extra virgin olive oil

- 4 tablespoons of balsamic vinegar

- 3 tablespoons of maple syrup

- 1 tablespoon Dijon mustard

- Salt and pepper to taste

Directions:

1. Preheat the oven to 400°F (200°C).

2. Place the butternut squash cubes on a baking sheet. Drizzle with olive oil, season with salt and pepper, and toss to coat evenly. Roast in the preheated oven for 20-25 minutes or until the squash is tender and lightly browned. Set aside to cool.

3. In a large salad bowl, combine the sliced kale, dried cranberries, toasted pumpkin seeds, and crumbled feta cheese. Set aside.

4. In a small bowl, whisk together the balsamic vinegar, maple syrup, Dijon mustard, minced

garlic, olive oil, salt, and pepper until well combined.

5. Add the cooled roasted butternut squash to the salad bowl with kale. Drizzle the maple-balsamic dressing over the salad and toss to coat all the Ingredients: evenly.

6. Allow the salad to sit for about 10 minutes to let the flavours meld together.

7. Serve the Butternut Squash and Kale Salad with Maple-Balsamic Dressing as a side dish or a light lunch.

Grilled Portobello Burger With Avocado Aioli

Ingredients:

- 2 ripe avocado

- 1/4 cup mayonnaise

- 2 clove of garlic, minced

- 2 tablespoon of lemon juice

- 1 tablespoon olive oil

- Four large Portobello mushroom caps

- Four burger buns

- Salt and pepper to taste

- Optional toppings: lettuce, tomato slices, red onion slices

Directions:

1. Preheat your grill to medium heat.

2. Prepare the Portobello mushrooms by removing the stems and gently brushing off any dirt. If desired, you can also remove the gills from the undersides of the mushrooms using a spoon.

3. In a small bowl, mash the avocado until smooth. Add the mayonnaise, minced garlic, lemon juice, olive oil, salt, and pepper. Mix well to combine and set aside.

4. Place the Portobello mushroom caps on the preheated grill, smooth side down. Cook for about 5-6 minutes or until the mushrooms start to soften and develop grill marks.

5. Flip the mushroom caps and continue grilling another 5-6 minutes or until they are tender and cooked through.

6. While the mushrooms are grilling, lightly toast the burger buns the grill or in a toaster.

7. Once the mushrooms are d2, remove them from the grill and let them cool slightly.

8. Spread a generous amount of the avocado aioli on the bottom half of each burger bun.

9. Place a grilled Portobello mushroom cap on top of the aioli.

10. Add your desired toppings, such as lettuce, tomato slices, and red onion.

11. Top the burger with the other half of the bun.

12. Serve the Grilled Portobello Burger with Avocado Aioli immediately, and enjoy!

Buddha Bowl

Ingredients:

- 1/2 cup shredded carrots

- 1/2 cup sliced cucumber

- 1/4 cup sliced radishes

- 1/4 cup chopped fresh cilantro

- 2 tablespoons tahini

- 1 tablespoon lemon juice

- 1 tablespoon water

- 1 cup cooked quinoa

- 1 cup roasted sweet potatoes, cubed

- 1 cup steamed broccoli florets

- 1 cup cooked chickpeas

- Salt and pepper to taste

Directions:

1. In a bowl, combine the cooked quinoa, roasted sweet potatoes, steamed broccoli florets, cooked chickpeas, shredded carrots, sliced cucumber, and sliced radishes.
2. In a separate small bowl, whisk together the tahini, lemon juice, water, salt, and pepper to create a dressing.
3. Drizzle the dressing over the Buddha bowl and toss to coat the Ingredients: evenly.
4. Sprinkle with fresh cilantro for added flavor and garnish.
5. Serve the Pegan Buddha bowl as a complete and satisfying meal.

Lemon Herb Grilled Chicken With Roasted Vegetables

Ingredients:

- 2 cloves garlic, minced

- 1 teaspoon dried oregano

- 1 teaspoon dried thyme

- Salt and pepper to taste

- Assorted vegetables for roasting (e.g., carrots, Brussels sprouts, bell peppers)

- 2 b2less, skinless chicken breasts

- Juice of 1 lemon

- 2 tablespoons olive oil

- Fresh herbs for garnish (e.g., parsley, basil)

Directions:

1. In a bowl, whisk together the lemon juice, olive oil, minced garlic, dried oregano, dried thyme, salt, and pepper to create a marinade.
2. Place the chicken breasts in a shallow dish and pour the marinade over them. Let the chicken marinate for at least 30 minutes, or ideally, overnight in the refrigerator.
3. Preheat the grill to medium-high heat.
4. Remove the chicken from the marinade and discard the excess marinade.
5. Grill the chicken breasts for about 6-8 minutes per side, or until cooked through and juices run clear.
6. While the chicken is grilling, prepare the roasted vegetables.
7. Toss the vegetables in olive oil, salt, and pepper, then spread them on a baking sheet. Roast in a preheated oven at 400°F (200°C) for 20-25 minutes or until tender and slightly caramelized.

8. Remove the chicken from the grill and let it rest for a few minutes before slicing.

9. Serve the grilled chicken alongside the roasted vegetables.

10. Garnish with fresh herbs for an extra burst of flavor.

Cauliflower Fried Rice

Ingredients:

- 1 small onion, diced

- 2 cloves garlic, minced

- 1 cup mixed vegetables (e.g., peas, carrots, bell peppers)

- 2 tablespoons tamari or soy sauce (gluten-free if desired)

- 2 green onions, sliced

- 1 small head of cauliflower, grated or finely chopped

- 1 tablespoon coconut oil

- Salt and pepper to taste

- Optional toppings: chopped cashews, sesame seeds, sliced avocado

Directions:

1. In a large skillet or wok, heat the coconut oil over medium heat.
2. Add the diced onion and minced garlic to the skillet and sauté until the onion is translucent.
3. Add the mixed vegetables to the skillet and stir-fry for a few minutes until they start to soften.
4. Push the vegetables to 2 side of the skillet and add the grated cauliflower to the other side.
5. Cook the cauliflower for 5-6 minutes, stirring occasionally, until it becomes tender.
6. Mix the cauliflower with the vegetables in the skillet.
7. Stir in the tamari or soy sauce and season with salt and pepper to taste.
8. Add the sliced green onions and cook for another minute.

9. Remove from heat and serve the cauliflower
    fried rice.

10. Top with chopped cashews, sesame seeds,
    and sliced avocado if desired.

Eggplant And Quinoa Stuffed Peppers

Ingredients:

- 3 cloves garlic, minced

- 2 tablespoons olive oil

- 1 teaspoon dried basil

- 1 teaspoon dried oregano

- 1 teaspoon dried thyme

- Salt and pepper to taste

- .1/4 cup grated Parmesan cheese (optional)

- 4 bell peppers (any colour)

- 1 cup quinoa

- . 2 cups water

- 1 eggplant, diced

- 1 onion, diced

Directions:

1. Preheat the oven to 375°F.

2. Cut off the tops of the bell peppers and remove the seeds and membranes. Place the peppers in a baking dish and set aside.

3. In a medium saucepan, combine the quinoa and water. Bring to a boil, then reduce the heat and simmer for 15-20 minutes, or until the quinoa is cooked and the water has been absorbed.

4. While the quinoa is cooking, heat the olive oil in a large skillet over medium heat. Add the eggplant, onion, and garlic and sauté until the vegetables are soft and the eggplant is tender.

5. Add the basil, oregano, thyme, salt, and
    pepper to the skillet and stir to combine. Add
    the cooked quinoa to the skillet and mix well.

6. Spoon the quinoa and eggplant mixture into
    the bell peppers, filling each pepper to the
    top. If desired, sprinkle Parmesan cheese on
    top of each pepper.

7. Cover the baking dish with foil and bake for
    35-40 minutes, or until the peppers are
    tender.

Roasted Red Pepper, Avocado And Arugula Salad

Ingredients:

- 2 cups arugula

- 1 tbsp olive oil

- 1 tbsp balsamic vinegar

- 1 large red bell pepper

- 1 avocado

- Salt and pepper to taste

Directions:

1. Preheat the oven to 450°F (232°C). Line a baking sheet with parchment paper.
2. Cut the red pepper into quarters and remove the stem and seeds. Place the pepper quarters on the prepared baking sheet.

3. Roast the red pepper in the preheated oven for 20-25 minutes or until the skin is charred and the flesh is soft. Remove the pepper from the oven and let it cool.

4. Once the pepper is cool enough to handle, peel off the skin and slice the flesh into thin strips.

5. Cut the avocado in half and remove the pit. Slice the avocado flesh into thin pieces.

6. In a small bowl, whisk together the olive oil, balsamic vinegar, salt, and pepper.

7. In a large bowl, toss the arugula with the dressing.

8. Add the roasted red pepper and avocado to the arugula and toss gently to combine.

9. Serve the salad immediately.

Coconut Curry Soup

Ingredients:

- 1 can (14 oz) full-fat coconut milk

- 1 cup diced sweet potato

- 1 cup diced carrots

- 1 cup sliced mushrooms

- 1/2 cup diced red bell pepper

- 1/2 cup chopped fresh cilantro

- Salt and pepper to taste

- Lime wedges, for serving (optional)

- 2 tablespoons coconut oil

- 1 medium onion, diced

- 3 cloves garlic, minced

- 2 tablespoons curry powder

- 1 teaspoon ground turmeric

- 1 teaspoon ground coriander

- 1/2 teaspoon ground cumin

- 1/4 teaspoon red pepper flakes

- 4 cups vegetable broth

Directions:

1. In a large pot or Dutch oven, heat the coconut oil over medium heat.
2. Add the onion and garlic and cook until softened, about 5 minutes.
3. Add the curry powder, turmeric, coriander, cumin, and red pepper flakes and cook for another 1-2 minutes until fragrant.
4. Add the vegetable broth, coconut milk, sweet potato, carrots, mushrooms, and red bell pepper. Stir to combine and bring to a boil.

5. Reduce the heat and simmer for 20-25 minutes until the vegetables are tender.

6. Stir in the cilantro and season with salt and pepper to taste.

7. Serve hot with lime wedges, if desired.

Mushroomlet

Ingredients:

- ¼ c. coconut milk

- ½ tsp. salt

- 8 eggs

- 3 c. button mushrooms

- ½ tsp. black pepper

- 1 chopped small onion

- Rapeseed oil

Directions:

1. In small bowl, whisk eggs in a bowl and reserve. Cut the mushrooms into fine slices and combine with onion, seasonings, and coconut.

2. Set a skillet over medium heat and heat 2
    teaspoons rapeseed oil over medium-high
    heat. Add onion and mushrooms, and sauté
    for 3 minutes until the onions are tender.
3. Add whisked eggs and cook for 6 minutes on
    both sides.
4. Serve warm and enjoy.

Banana Chocolate Pancakes

Ingredients:

- Organic honey

- ¼ c. coconut flour

- 2 eggs

- 1 c. almond milk

- ¼ tsp. salt

- 1 tsp. baking powder

- 2 bananas

- ¼ c. cocoa

- Coconut oil

Directions:

1. In medium bowl, whisk eggs and combine
   vanilla extract, almond milk, 2 tablespoons
   honey, 1 tablespoon coconut oil, and salt in a
   bowl.
2. Set up a second bowl to sift coconut flour and
   baking powder.
3. Slowly add wet mixture into dry mixture while
   mixing.
4. Lightly smear a skillet with coconut oil and put
   over medium heat.
5. Pour approximately ¼ cup of batter into skillet
   and cook approximately 2 minutes per side.
   Flip the pancakes over when little bubbles
   form.
6. Cut the bananas into slices and serve as a
   topping of pancakes with a drizzle of h2y.

Citrus Apple Smoothie

Ingredients:

- 1½ c. chilled filtered water

- 1 peeled, cored and chopped large apple

- ½ tbsp. fresh lemon juice

- ½ tsp. freshly grated lemon zest

- 1 peeled, seeded and sectioned large orange

Directions:

1. Blend all the Ingredients: until smooth in a high-speed blender.
2. Put the mixture into 2 large serving glasses.
3. Serve immediately and enjoy.

Best Spicy Egg Salad Recipe

INGREDIENTS:

- 2 tablespoons mayonnaise

- 2 teaspoons Sriracha sauce

- 1 teaspoon chili paste Sambal Oelek or other brand

- 1/4 teaspoon salt

- 1/4 teaspoon black pepper

- 6 eggs large

- 6 slices bacon cooked and crumbled

- 2 tablespoons onion sweet onion variety, finely chopped

- 2 tablespoons Greek yogurt

- 1 teaspoon sugar

DIRECTIONS:

1. Carefully place large eggs single layer in a pot of cold water.

2. Bring the pot to a rolling boil.

3. Take off heat, cover and let stand on the burner for 12 to 15 minutes

4. Drain the hot water from the pan and fill with cool water and some ice. When the hard-boiled eggs are cool, chop them into small even size pieces. Set eggs aside.

5. While your eggs are boiling cook bacon until crisp, drain, and pat excess grease off. Crumble the bacon in to small pieces and set aside.

6. Chop sweet onion into small even size pieces then set aside.

7. In a large bowl, combine mayonnaise, Greek yogurt, Sriacha, chili paste, salt, pepper, and sugar. Mix until it has a smooth creamy consistency.

8. Add the remaining ingredients, chopped eggs, bacon, and onions. The last thing, gently stir to mix the egg salad together.

Green Jacket Salad

INGREDIENTS:

SALAD:

- 1/4 cup tomatoes cherry tomatoes cut in 1/2 or diced tomatoes

- 1/3 cup pita chips broken into bite-size pieces

- 2 tablespoons parmesan cheese freshly grated to topping

- 1 1/2 cups Romaine lettuce washed and torn into biz-size pieces

- 1 1/2 cups leaf lettuce washed and torn into biz-size pieces

DRESSING:

- 1/2 teaspoon season salt I like Lawrys for this recipe

- 2 green onions finly sliced from the white part all the way up to the top of the green

- 2 teaspoons parsley fresh, finely chopped

- 2 tablespoons olive oil

- 2 tablespoons red wine vinegar

- 1 teaspoon oregano dried

DIRECTIONS:

DRESSING:

1. Combine all dressing Ingredients: into a glass jar. Screw on a tight-fitting lid. Shake until all ingredients are combined.

SALAD:

2. Combine lettuce and tomatoes in a medium-size bowl

3. Pour dressing over salad and toss

4. Add pita chips and toss lightly.

5. Top with parmesan cheese if desired

Greek Wedge Salad

INGREDIENTS:

- 1 teaspoon oregano dried

- 1 teaspoon salt

- 1 teaspoon black pepper

- 6 tablespoons red wine vinegar

- 2 tablespoons Dijon mustard

- 2 tablespoons h2y

- 1/2 cup olive oil

- 1 cup chickpeas rinsed and drained

- 1 cup English cucumber chopped

- 1 cup Roma tomato chopped

- 1/4 cup Kalamata olives halved pitted

- 1/4 cup red onion finely chopped

- 1/4 cup flatleaf parsley chopped fresh

- 4 romaine lettuce hearts hearts, cut in half lengthwise

DIRECTIONS:

1. Combine chickpeas, cucumber, tomato, olives and red onion in a medium-size bowl.

2. In a glass jar add parsley, oregano, salt, pepper, vinegar, mustard, honey, and olive oil. Seal with a tight fitting lid and shake for a minute until all ingredients are blended well.

3. Toss half of dressing with chopped vegetables in a bowl.

4. Place romaine halves on plates and spoon chopped vegetables over the hearts. Drizzle the remaining dressing evenly over romaine hearts.

Almond Butter Energy Balls

Ingredients:

- 1/four cup h2y or maple syrup (regulate sweetness to your liking)

- 1/four cup unsweetened shredded coconut 1/four cup flour flaxseed

- 1/four cup mini darkish chocolate chips or chopped nuts (elective)

- 1 teaspoon vanilla extract

- 1 cup rolled oats

- half of a cup almond butter (ideally herbal and unsweetened)

- Pinch of salt

Directions:

1. In a meals processor or blender, pulse the
    rolled oats till they're damaged down into a
    rough texture.
2. In a big blending bowl, integrate the almond
    butter, h2y, maple syrup, shredded coconut,
    floor flaxseed, chocolate chips or nuts (if the
    usage of), vanilla extract, and salt. Mix nicely
    till all of the comp2nts are lightly combined.
3. Add the pulsed oats to the combination bowl
    and stir till the aggregate will become sticky
    and nicely incorporated.
4. Place the combination with inside the fridge
    for approximately 15-half-hour to cooperate
    up barely, because it will make it less difficult
    to roll into balls.
5. Once chilled, take small quantities of the
    combination and roll them among your arms
    to shape compact balls. Adjust the dimensions
    in step with your preference.

6. Repeat the procedure till all the combinations are used. If preferred, you could roll the power balls in extra shredded coconut or floor flaxseed for additional texture and taste.

7. Store the almond butter strength balls in a hermetic box inside the fridge for up to 2 weeks. They also can be frozen for longer storage.

8. These almond butter power balls make a handy on-the-move snack and are high-quality for pleasing your candy enamel even as imparting a lift of sustained power.

9. You can experience them earlier than or after an exercise, as a mid-afternoon pick-me-up, or on every occasion you want a wholesome and scrumptious snack.

10. Feel free to customize the recipe with the aid of using different substances like chia seeds, dried result, or spices along with cinnamon or nutmeg. Enjoy!

Kale Chips

Ingredients:

- 1-2 tablespoons olive oil

- Salt, to flavor

- 1 bunch of kale

- Optional seasonings: garlic powder, paprika, dietary yeast, or every other favored spice

Directions:

1. Preheat your oven to 350°F (175°C).
2. Wash the kale very well and pat it dry with a paper towel or use a salad spinner to cast off extra moisture.
3. Make certain the kale leaves are absolutely dry; otherwise, they might not turn out to be crispy.
4. Remove the kale leaves from the hard middle stems via means of tearing or reducing them

into bite-sized pieces. Discard the stems or store them for different recipes like smoothies or stir-fries.

5. In a huge bowl, drizzle the kale leaves with olive oil. Use your palms to rubdown the oil onto the leaves, making sure they're calmly lined.

6. Sprinkle salt and any preferred seasonings over the kale leaves. Toss lightly to distribute the seasonings.

7. Arrange the kale leaves in an unmarried layer on a baking sheet covered with parchment paper or a silic2 mat.

8. Place the baking sheet with inside the preheated oven and bake for approximately 10-15 minutes, or till the kale leaves are crispy and barely golden. Keep an eye fixed on them as they could quickly burn.

    Remove the kale chips from the oven and

allow them to cool on the baking sheet for a couple of minutes to crisp up further.

9. Transfer the kale chips to a bowl or a plate, and they may be geared up to be loved.

10. You can delight in the kale chips right now or save them in a hermetic box for some days.

11. However, keep in mind that the longer they sit, the less crispy they'll come to be. Kale chips make an awesome guilt-unfastened snack, full of fiber, nutrients A and K, and diverse different nutrients.

12. They provide a fulfilling crunch and may be good to fit your flavor choices. Experiment with exclusive spices or strive to sprinkle a few dietary yeasts for a tacky taste.

13. Enjoy those self-made kale chips as a wholesome opportunity to normal chips or as a satisfying addition to your lunchbox or birthday celebration platter.

Eggplant And Quinoa Stuffed Peppers

Ingredients:

- 1 eggplant, diced

- 1 onion, diced

- 3 cloves garlic, minced

- 2 tablespoons olive oil

- 1 teaspoon dried basil

- 1 teaspoon dried oregano

- 1 teaspoon dried thyme

- 4 bell peppers (any colour)

- 1 cup quinoa

- 2 cups water

- Salt and pepper to taste

- 1/4 cup grated Parmesan cheese (optional)

Directions:

1. Preheat the oven to 375°F.
2. Cut off the tops of the bell peppers and remove the seeds and membranes. Place the peppers in a baking dish and set aside.
3. In a medium saucepan, combine the quinoa and water. Bring to a boil, then reduce the heat and simmer for 15-20 minutes, or until the quinoa is cooked and the water has been absorbed.
4. While the quinoa is cooking, heat the olive oil in a large skillet over medium heat. Add the eggplant, onion, and garlic and sauté until the vegetables are soft and the eggplant is tender.
5. Add the basil, oregano, thyme, salt, and pepper to the skillet and stir to combine. Add the cooked quinoa to the skillet and mix well.
6. Spoon the quinoa and eggplant mixture into the bell peppers, filling each pepper to the

top. If desired, sprinkle Parmesan cheese on top of each pepper.

7. Cover the baking dish with foil and bake for 35-40 minutes, or until the peppers are tender.

Roasted Red Pepper, Avocado And Arugula Salad

Ingredients:

- 2 cups arugula

- 1 tbsp olive oil

- 1 tbsp balsamic vinegar

- 1 large red bell pepper

- 1 avocado

- Salt and pepper to taste

Directions:

1. Preheat the oven to 450°F (232°C). Line a baking sheet with parchment paper.

2. Cut the red pepper into quarters and remove the stem and seeds. Place the pepper quarters on the prepared baking sheet.

3. Roast the red pepper in the preheated oven for 20-25 minutes or until the skin is charred and the flesh is soft. Remove the pepper from the oven and let it cool.

4. Once the pepper is cool enough to handle, peel off the skin and slice the flesh into thin strips.

5. Cut the avocado in half and remove the pit. Slice the avocado flesh into thin pieces.

6. In a small bowl, whisk together the olive oil, balsamic vinegar, salt, and pepper.

7. In a large bowl, toss the arugula with the dressing.

8. Add the roasted red pepper and avocado to the arugula and toss gently to combine.

9. Serve the salad immediately.

Coconut Curry Soup

Ingredients:

- 1 teaspoon ground coriander

- 1/2 teaspoon ground cumin

- 1/4 teaspoon red pepper flakes

- 4 cups vegetable broth

- 1 can (14 oz) full-fat coconut milk

- 1 cup diced sweet potato

- 1 cup diced carrots

- 1 cup sliced mushrooms

- 1/2 cup diced red bell pepper

- 1/2 cup chopped fresh cilantro

- 2 tablespoons coconut oil

- 1 medium onion, diced

- 3 cloves garlic, minced

- 2 tablespoons curry powder

- 1 teaspoon ground turmeric

- Salt and pepper to taste

- Lime wedges, for serving (optional)

Directions:

1. In a large pot or Dutch oven, heat the coconut oil over medium heat.

2. Add the onion and garlic and cook until softened, about 5 minutes.

3. Add the curry powder, turmeric, coriander, cumin, and red pepper flakes and cook for another 1-2 minutes until fragrant.

4. Add the vegetable broth, coconut milk, sweet potato, carrots, mushrooms, and red bell pepper. Stir to combine and bring to a boil.

5. Reduce the heat and simmer for 20-25
    minutes until the vegetables are tender.

6. Stir in the cilantro and season with salt and
    pepper to taste.

7. Serve hot with lime wedges, if desired.

Eggplant And Quinoa Stuffed Peppers

Ingredients:

- 3 cloves garlic, minced

- 2 tablespoons olive oil

- 1 teaspoon dried basil

- 1 teaspoon dried oregano

- 1 teaspoon dried thyme

- 4 bell peppers (any colour)

- 1 cup quinoa

- 2 cups water

- 1 eggplant, diced

- 1 onion, diced

- Salt and pepper to taste

- 1/4 cup grated Parmesan cheese (optional)

Directions:

1. Preheat the oven to 375°F.

2. Cut off the tops of the bell peppers and remove the seeds and membranes. Place the peppers in a baking dish and set aside.

3. In a medium saucepan, combine the quinoa and water. Bring to a boil, then reduce the heat and simmer for 15-20 minutes, or until the quinoa is cooked and the water has been absorbed.

4. While the quinoa is cooking, heat the olive oil in a large skillet over medium heat. Add the eggplant, onion, and garlic and sauté until the vegetables are soft and the eggplant is tender.

5. Add the basil, oregano, thyme, salt, and pepper to the skillet and stir to combine. Add the cooked quinoa to the skillet and mix well.

6. Spoon the quinoa and eggplant mixture into the bell peppers, filling each pepper to the

top. If desired, sprinkle Parmesan cheese on
top of each pepper.

7. Cover the baking dish with foil and bake for
35-40 minutes, or until the peppers are
tender.

Healthy Coconut Granola

Ingredients:

- 1 Tbsp coconut sugar

- 1/4 tsp sea salt

- 3 Tbsp coconut oil

- 1/3 cup maple syrup

- 1 tsp pure vanilla extract

- 1 1/2 cups gluten-free rolled oats

- 1/2 cup unsweetened coconut flake (large flakes are best)

- 1/2 cup slivered raw almonds (or raw almonds, chopped)

- 1/2 cup raw pecan halves

- 1/4 cup dried fruit (my favorite is blueberry // optional)

Directions:

1. Preheat oven to 325 degrees F (162 C).

2. Add oats, coconut, almonds, pecans, coconut sugar, and salt to a large mixing bowl and stir to combine.

3. To a small saucepan, add coconut oil and maple syrup. Warm over medium heat for 2-3 minutes, whisking frequently until the 3 are totally combined and there is no visible separation. Add vanilla, whisk once more.

4. Immediately pour over the dry Ingredients: and stir to combine until all oats and nuts are thoroughly coated. Arrange on a parchment-lined large baking sheet and spread into an even layer.

5. Bake for 20 minutes, then remove from oven and turn the pan around so the other end goes into the oven first (so it bakes evenly).

6. To keep this granola chunky, don't stir during baking, or right after. This will help it form together and create "chunks", so handle as little as possible!

7. Bake 5-7 minutes more, watching carefully as to not let it burn. You'll know it's d2 when the granola is golden brown and very fragrant.

8. Let cool completely before enjoying. Add dried fruit to the pan while the granola is cooling (optional). Break into clumps.

9. Store in a sealed bag or container at room temperature for 2 weeks or in the freezer for up to 1 month.

10. This is delicious as is or with almond or coconut milk, flaxseed meal, hemp seeds, and banana!

Roasted Nuts And Seeds

Ingredients:

- 1 cup raw walnut pieces or halves

- 1 cup raw pecan pieces or halves

- 1 cup raw peanuts (or dry roasted without salt)

- 1 cup raw cashew pieces or halves

- 3/4 cup raw hazelnuts

- 1 cup raw sunflower seeds (or dry roasted without salt)

- 1 cup raw pumpkin seeds

- 2 cup raw almonds

- 1/2 cup pistachios, roasted and salted

Directions:

1. Roast nuts separately by type in single layer on cookie sheets lined with parchment paper or foil. Roast at 350 degrees for the following times:

2. Almonds - 20 minutes

3. Walnuts, pecans, hazelnuts - 15 minutes

4. Cashews, peanuts - 10 minutes

5. Sunflower and pumpkin - 5-7 minutes (can be added without roasting if you like)

6. Pistachio nuts - I have only found them roasted and salted, so they are the only added salt in this recipe.

Collard Green Breakfast Wraps

Ingredients:

FOR PICKLED RED ONIONS:

- 1 teaspoon sea salt

- 1 large red onion, thinly sliced

- ¾ cup (180 ml) apple cider vinegar

- 1 tablespoon (20 g) maple syrup

FOR COLLARD WRAPS:

- 2 large pastured eggs, scrambled

- 4 bacon slices, cooked

- ½ cup (80 g) pickled red onions

- Salsa, for dipping

- 4 collard greens

- 1 cup (256 g) black beans

- ½ avocado, peeled and sliced

Directions:

1. To make the pickled onions: In a small saucepan over medium heat, combine the vinegar, maple syrup, and salt. Bring the mixture to a low simmer.

2. Place the sliced red onion in a jar or small container and pour the hot vinegar mixture over the top. Let soak for at least 1 hour, or refrigerate overnight.

3. To make the collard wraps: Soak the collard leaves in warm water for 20 minutes while preparing the filling Ingredients:.

4. Cut the protruding side of the collard leaf stem off the inner side of each leaf and trim off the stem at the bottom of the leaf.

5. Place 3 leaves, side by side, stem-side up, with the 3 stem ends overlapping each other. Into

the center of the leaves, place half each of the
black beans, avocado, eggs, bacon, and
pickled red onions.

6. Fold both top ends of the leaves to the center,
covering the fillings. Similar to wrapping a
burrito, fold 2 side to the center and roll up
the bundle.

7. Repeat with the remaining leaves and filling.
Halve the wraps and serve with salsa for
dipping.

8. Refrigerate leftover pickled red onions in an
airtight container for up to 1 week.

Friendly Leek And Herb Gravy

Ingredients:

- ¼ cup all-purpose gluten free rice flour blend

- 1 teaspoon finely diced Italian oregano

- 1 teaspoon finely diced lemon thyme

- 2/3 cup diced leek

- 1 cup dry white wine

- 2 cups chicken stock or water

- 1 teaspoon finely diced rosemary

Directions:

1. To skillet add flour, stirring frequently, and toast 1 minute (will become fragrant and a light brown).

2. Whisk in stock/water, wine, and diced leeks.

3. Bring to a boil, cover, reduce heat and simmer
    25-30 minutes or until reduced by half. Stir
    occasionally.

4. Stir in diced oregano, thyme, and rosemary.

Cold Busting Soup

Ingredients:

- 1 cup shiitake mushrooms, sliced

- 1-inch fresh ginger, diced OR 1 teaspoon ground ginger

- 1-inch fresh turmeric, diced OR 1 teaspoon of ground turmeric

- ½ tsp peppercorns

- 4 cups shredded chicken meat

- 1 tablespoon Beau Monde seasoning

- 1 bouquet of herbs*

- 1/3 cup matchstick carrots

- 6-8 cups b2 stock

Directions:

1. In pot combine Beau Monde seasoning, herbs, matchstick carrots, ginger, turmeric, peppercorns, chicken, stock

2. Bring to a boil, cover, reduce heat and let simmer 10-15 minutes.

3. Bouquet of herb is a bunch of herbs tied together mount per serving

Cauliflower Steaks With Walnuts And Pomegranate

Ingredients:

- ¼ cup walnuts

- ¼ cup pomegranates

- 4 basil leaves, coarsely chopped

- 4 cauliflower steaks

- Olive oil for drizzling

- Pumpkin or soy seeds (optional)

Directions:

1. Preheat oven to 350 and line baking tray with parchment paper.

2. Lay steaks on tray, drizzle with oil and sprinkle with walnuts and pomegranates. Bake 10-15 minutes.

3. Top with pieces of basil and seeds before
   serving!

Grilled Zucchini Meal

Ingredients:

- 1 teaspoon paprika

- 1 teaspoon garlic powder

- 1 tablespoon of sea salt

- 1-2 stevia

- Olive oil as needed

- 3 zucchinis

- ½ teaspoon black pepper

- ½ teaspoon mustard

- ½ teaspoon cumin

- 1 tablespoon chilli powder

Directions:

1. Preheat your oven to 300 degrees F

2. Take a small bowl and add cayenne, black pepper, salt, garlic, mustard, paprika, chilli powder, and stevia

3. Mix well

4. Slice zucchini into 1/8 inch slices and mist them with olive oil

5. Sprinkle spice blend over Zucchini and bake for 40 minutes

6. Remove and flip, mist with more olive oil and leftover spice

7. Bake for 20 minutes more

8. Serve!

Garlic And Kale Platter

Ingredients:

- 1 bunch kale

- 2 tablespoons olive oil

- 4 garlic cloves, minced

Directions:

1. Carefully tear the kale into bite-sized portions, making sure to remove the stem
2. Discard the stems
3. Take a large-sized pot and place it over medium heat
4. Add olive oil and let the oil heat up
5. Add garlic and stir for 2 minutes
6. Add kale and cook for 5-10 minutes
7. Serve!

Healthy Guacamole

Ingredients:

- 4 tablespoon of freshly squeezed lime juice

- Salt as needed

- Freshly ground black pepper as needed

- 3 large ripe avocados

- 1 large red onion, peeled and diced

- Cayenne pepper as needed

Directions:

1. Halve the avocados and discard the st2
2. Scoop flesh from 3 avocado halves and transfer to a large bowl
3. Mash using fork
4. Add 2 tablespoon of lime juice and mix

5. Dice the remaining avocado flesh (remaining half) and transfer to another bowl

6. Add remaining juice and toss

7. Add diced flesh with the mashed flesh and mix

8. Add chopped onions and toss

9. Season with salt, pepper, and cayenne pepper

10. Serve and enjoy!

Savory Oatmeal Porridge

Ingredients:

- 1 tablespoon faro

- 1/2 cup slivered almonds

- 1/4 cup Nutritional yeast

- 2 cups old-fashi2d rolled oats

- 2 1/2 cups vegetable broth

- 2 1/2 cups milk

- 1/2 cup steel-cut oats

- 1/2 teaspoon salt (optional)

Directions:

1. Take the broth and almond milk to a boil. Add the oats, faro, almond slivers, and Nutritional

yeast. Cook over medium-high heat for 20 minutes, stirring occasionally.

2. Add the rolled oats and cook for another 5 minutes, until creamy. Stir in the salt (if using).

3. Divide into four single-serving containers. Let cool before sealing the lids.

Mango And Kale Smoothie

Ingredients:

- ½ cup kale leaves

- 2 teaspoons coconut sugar

- 1 cup mango pieces

- 2 cups oats milk, unsweetened

- 2 bananas, peeled

- 1 teaspoon vanilla extract, unsweetened

Directions:

1. In the container of a high-speed food processor or blender, combine all of the Ingredients: in the order specified in the Ingredients: list and then cover with the lid.

2. Pulse for 1 minute until smooth, and then serve.

Pomegranate Smoothie

Ingredients:

- 2 bananas, peeled

- 2 cups frozen raspberries

- 1 cup pomegranate seeds

- 2 cups almond milk, unsweetened

- 2 medium apples, cored, sliced

- 4 teaspoons agave syrup

Directions:

1. In the container of a high-speed food processor or blender, combine all of the Ingredients: in the order specified in the Ingredients: list and then cover with the lid.
2. Pulse for 1 minute until smooth, and then serve.

Golden Turmeric Latte

Ingredients:

- ½ teaspoon ground cinnamon

- ½ teaspoon ground ginger

- 1 teaspoon maple syrup or h2y

- 1 cup of almond milk (or other plant-based milk)

- 1 teaspoon ground turmeric

- Pinch of black pepper

Directions:

1. In a small saucepan, heat almond milk over medium heat until warmed but not boiling.

2. Whisk in ground turmeric, cinnamon, ginger, maple syrup or h2y, and a pinch of black pepper.

3. Continue whisking until well combined and
    heated through.

4. Pour into a mug and savor the warm and
    comforting flavors of this golden turmeric
    latte.

Roasted Brussels Sprouts With Balsamic Glaze

Ingredients:

- 2 tablespoons olive oil

- Salt and pepper to taste

- 1 pound Brussels sprouts, peeled and halved

- 2 tablespoons balsamic glaze

Directions:

1. Preheat the oven to 400°F (200°C).
2. In a mixing bowl, toss Brussels sprouts with olive oil, salt, and pepper until well coated.
3. Spread the Brussels sprouts in a single layer on a baking sheet.
4. Roast in the oven for 20-25 minutes, or until they are tender and lightly browned.
5. Drizzle balsamic glaze over the roasted Brussels sprouts and toss to coat.

6. Transfer to a serving dish and serve as a
    flavorful and nutritious side dish.

Cauliflower Mash

Ingredients:

- 2 cloves garlic, minced

- 2 tablespoons olive oil

- ¼ cup vegetable broth

- 1 medium head cauliflower, cut into florets

- Salt and pepper to taste

- Fresh chives for garnish

Directions:

1. 1 medium cauliflower head, florets

2. In a skillet, heat olive oil over medium heat. Sauté the minced garlic until fragrant.

3. Transfer the cooked cauliflower to a food processor or blender.

4. Add sautéed garlic, vegetable broth, salt, and pepper.

5. Blend until smooth and creamy, adjusting the consistency with additional vegetable broth if needed.

6. Transfer the cauliflower mash to a serving bowl, garnish with fresh chives, and serve as a delicious and healthier alternative to traditional mashed potatoes.

Quinoa And Vegetable Stir-Fry

Ingredients:

- 3 carrots, thinly sliced

- 2 zucchini, thinly sliced

- 1 cup broccoli florets

- 1 cup snap peas

- 4 tablespoons soy sauce

- 2 tablespoon of sesame oil

- 2 tablespoon of rice vinegar

- 1 cup quinoa

- 2 cups water

- 2 tablespoons vegetable oil

- 4 cloves garlic, minced

- 2 small onion, diced

- 1 bell pepper, thinly sliced

- Salt and pepper to taste

- Optional toppings: chopped green onions, sesame seeds

Directions:

1. Rinse the quinoa under cold water and drain. In a medium-sized saucepan, bring the water to a boil.

2. Add the quinoa, reduce the heat to low, cover, and simmer for about 15 minutes or until the quinoa is cooked and the water is absorbed.

3. Remove from heat and let it sit, covered, for 5 minutes. Fluff the quinoa with a fork and set aside.

4. heat the vegetable oil over medium-high heat in a large skillet or wok.

5. Add the bell pepper, carrots, zucchini, broccoli florets, and snap peas to the skillet. Stir-fry the vegetables for about 5-6 minutes until they are crisp-tender but retain their vibrant colors.

6. Mix the Ingredients: in a low-volume dish using a whisk. soy sauce, sesame oil, rice

vinegar, salt, and pepper. Pour the sauce over
the vegetables in the skillet and stir to coat
evenly.

7. Add the cooked quinoa to the skillet Cook for
an additional 2-3 minutes to heat the quinoa
through.

8. Remove the stir-fry from the heat and serve
hot. You can garnish it with chopped green
onions and sesame seeds if desired.

Roasted Beet And Goat Cheese Salad

Ingredients:

- 4 ounces goat cheese, crumbled

- 1/2 cup walnuts, toasted and chopped

- 3 tablespoons of balsamic vinegar

- 3 tablespoons extra-virgin olive oil

- Four medium-sized beets

- 4 cups mixed salad greens

- Salt and pepper to taste

Directions:

1. Preheat your oven to 400°F (200°C).
2. Trim off the beet greens and scrub the beets to remove dirt.

3. Place the beets on a baking sheet and drizzle them with olive oil. Season with salt and pepper.

4. Roast the beets in the preheated oven for about 45 minutes or until they are tender when pierced with a fork.

5. Once the beets are cooked, remove them from the oven and let them cool for a few minutes.

6. Once the beets are cool enough to handle, peel off the skins. They should come off quickly.

7. Cut the roasted beets into bite-sized wedges or slices.

8. In a large salad bowl, combine the mixed salad greens, roasted beet wedges, crumbled goat cheese, and toasted walnuts.

9. whisk the balsamic vinegar and extra-virgin olive oil in a small bowl. Season with salt and pepper to taste.

10. Drizzle the dressing over the salad and toss
    gently to coat all the Ingredients:.

11. Serve the roasted beet and goat cheese salad
    immediately.

Sweet Potato And Chickpea Buddha Bowl

Ingredients:

- 4 cups cooked quinoa or rice

- 2 cups baby spinach or mixed greens

- 1/2 cup cherry tomatoes, halved

- 1/2 cup cucumber, diced

- 1/4 cup red onion, thinly sliced

- 1/4 cup fresh cilantro, chopped

- 1/4 cup unsalted roasted peanuts, chopped (optional)

- 3 large sweet potatoes peeled and cut into cubes

- 2 can (15 ounces) of chickpeas, drained and rinsed

- 2 tablespoon of olive oil

- 2 teaspoon of ground cumin

- 2 teaspoon of smoked paprika

- 1/2 teaspoon garlic powder

- Salt and pepper to taste

- Lemon wedges for serving

Directions:

1. Preheat the oven to 425°F (220°C).

2. In a large bowl, combine the sweet potato cubes, chickpeas, olive oil, cumin, smoked paprika, garlic powder, salt, and pepper. Toss until the sweet potatoes and chickpeas are evenly coated with the spices.

3. Spread the sweet potato and chickpea mixture in a single layer on a baking sheet. Bake in the preheated oven for about 25-30

minutes or until the sweet potatoes are tender and golden brown.

4. While the sweet potatoes and chickpeas are roasting, prepare the remaining Ingredients:. Cook the quinoa or rice according to package instructions.

5. In serving bowls, divide the cooked quinoa or rice, baby spinach or mixed greens, cherry tomatoes, cucumber, and red onion.

6. Once the sweet potatoes and chickpeas are cooked, remove them from the oven and let them cool slightly.

7. Add the roasted sweet potatoes and chickpeas to the serving bowls.

8. Sprinkle with fresh cilantro and chopped peanuts (if using).

9. Serve the Sweet Potato and Chickpea Buddha Bowl with lemon wedges on the side for squeezing over the bowl.

10. Enjoy your nutritious and delicious Sweet
Potato and Chickpea Buddha Bowl!

Quinoa And Vegetable Stuffed Bell Peppers

Ingredients:

- 1 cup diced zucchini

- 1 cup diced eggplant

- 1 cup diced tomatoes

- 1/4 cup chopped fresh basil

- 1/4 cup chopped fresh parsley

- 1 tablespoon olive oil

- 4 large bell peppers (assorted colors)

- 1 cup cooked quinoa

- 1 small onion, diced

- 2 cloves garlic, minced

- Salt and pepper to taste

Directions:

1.   Preheat the oven to 375°F (190°C).

2.   Cut the tops off the bell peppers and remove the seeds and membranes.

3.   Place the bell peppers in a baking dish, cut side up.

4.   In a skillet, heat the olive oil over medium heat.

5.   Add the onion and garlic to the skillet and sauté until the onion is translucent.

6.   Add the diced zucchini and eggplant to the skillet and cook for 5-7 minutes until slightly softened.

7.   Stir in the diced tomatoes, cooked quinoa, chopped basil, and chopped parsley. Season with salt and pepper.

8.   Spoon the quinoa and vegetable mixture into the bell peppers, filling them to the top.

9.   Cover the baking dish with foil and bake for 25-30 minutes until the peppers are tender.

10. Remove from the oven and let cool for a few

minutes before serving.

Lentil And Vegetable Curry

Ingredients:

- 1 tablespoon curry powder

- 1 teaspoon ground cumin

- 1 teaspoon ground turmeric

- 1/2 teaspoon ground ginger

- 1 cup diced tomatoes

- 1 cup vegetable broth

- 2 cups chopped mixed vegetables (e.g., cauliflower, bell peppers, carrots)

- 1 cup coconut milk

- 1 cup dried lentils (any variety), cooked according to package Directions:

- 1 tablespoon coconut oil

- 1 small onion, diced

- 2 cloves garlic, minced

- Salt and pepper to taste

- Fresh cilantro for garnish

Directions:

1. In a large pot or skillet, heat the coconut oil over medium heat.

2. Add the diced onion and minced garlic to the pot and sauté until the onion is translucent.

3. Stir in the curry powder, ground cumin, ground turmeric, and ground ginger. Cook for another minute to toast the spices.

4. Add the diced tomatoes and vegetable broth to the pot. Stir well to combine.

5. Bring the mixture to a simmer and add the chopped mixed vegetables.

6. Cover the pot and let the vegetables cook for about 10 minutes, or until tender.

7. Stir in the cooked lentils and coconut milk. Season with salt and pepper.

8. Let the curry simmer for another 5 minutes to allow the flavors to meld together.

9. Remove from heat and garnish with fresh cilantro.

10. Serve the lentil and vegetable curry over cooked quinoa or brown rice for a satisfying meal.

Avocado Cucumber Sushi Rolls

Ingredients:

- 1/4 cup shredded carrots

- 1/4 cup thinly sliced bell peppers (assorted colors)

- 2 tablespoons sesame seeds

- 2 large cucumbers

- 1 ripe avocado, sliced

- Tamari or soy sauce (gluten-free if desired), for dipping

Directions:

1. Cut the cucumbers lengthwise into thin strips using a vegetable peeler or a mandolin slicer.

2. Lay 2 cucumber strip flat on a clean surface and place a few slices of avocado, shredded carrots, and sliced bell peppers at 2 end.

3. Gently roll up the cucumber strip, enclosing the filling. Repeat with the remaining cucumber strips and filling Ingredients:.

4. Sprinkle the sesame seeds on a plate and roll the prepared sushi rolls in the seeds to coat them.

5. Serve the avocado cucumber sushi rolls with tamari or soy sauce for dipping.